THE GOSPEL IS FOR EVERYONE

The Gospel is for Everyone

BY

GRAHAM LEONARD

Bishop of Willesden

FOREWORD BY
THE ARCHBISHOP OF CANTERBURY

THE FAITH PRESS
7 Tufton Street, London, S.W.1
MOREHOUSE-BARLOW CO. INC., NEW YORK, U.S.A.

FIRST PUBLISHED IN 1971

PRINTED IN GREAT BRITAIN
in 10pt. Times type
BY THE FAITH PRESS LTD.
LEIGHTON BUZZARD
SBN 7164 0195 9

TO
PRISCILLA

CONTENTS

FOREWORD

MY first comment as I looked through this book was 'how beautifully short the chapters are'. Indeed most of the books which I have sponsored in this series contain six or seven chapters. But here are thirty-five. I like this plan. It helps those of us who do our reading only in small snatches; but those who are used to reading longer stretches at a time are compelled to pause and digest what each chapter gives us. And each of them gives us something to eat slowly and digest carefully as the diet of a great theme.

It is a book to ponder and to spend time in doing so. Its theme is that we should be better Christians, more Christlike, more good, more saintly than we are. But we do this not by struggling to follow an ethical example so much as by receiving a gift and realising our true status. While like all human beings we strive to justify ourselves to ourselves and to others, unconsciously ruled by all manner of thoughts of status in relation to the world around us, it is God who gives us our real status as His sons, and our Christian life is its faithful acceptance. Here is the meaning of Gospel, Church, sacraments, worship, prayer, practical Christian ethics. This book helps us to see many moments in our lives as illustrations of the true relationship. It is wide ranging in its applications while it retains a rare simplicity of theme.

I commend this book wholeheartedly to those who believe that renewal is the secret of unity and effective witness in the Christian Church, and renewal means to recapture in humility that relation to God which defines the Christian name.

✠ MICHAEL CANTUAR:

INTRODUCTION

AT the heart of the Gospel is the fact that God accepts us in Christ, setting us in a new and creative relationship to Himself. It follows that the Church must be the company of those who are learning to accept each other because they have been accepted by God. The Church on earth, if it is true to the Gospel, must be a 'mixed' society with room for the 'square' and the 'radical', the saint and the newly-converted, the plodder and the enthusiast, and must resist the pressure to become a sect. Further, the demands of Christian discipleship must be such as can be met by everyone.

I have had it in mind that this is a 'Lent Book'. While it can be read straight through, each chapter is complete in itself, and can be used as a basis for meditation each day. There are three underlying themes. The first is that the Christian life is a gift of God. It is not the result of man's effort. Secondly, the criteria by which someone is to be regarded as a practising Christian are very simple. They are possible for all, whatever may be our abilities, temperaments or intelligence, though utterly demanding in their implications. The third theme is that our effectiveness as ambassadors of the Gospel depends ultimately upon the quality of our lives. I believe that there is an urgent need for these points to be emphasised at the present day. Any time of reform brings with it a danger, namely, that reform is seen as an end in itself. Reform must go hand in hand with a renewal of Christian discipleship, and must not be regarded as a substitute for it. If this is not so, two things happen which undermine the life of the Church. First, the nature of holiness and Christian discipleship is forgotten. Commitment to this or that particular proposal for reform is wrongly regarded as the mark of the 'real' Churchman. Secondly, proposals for reform are not subjected to judgment in the light of the Gospel. The Church imperceptibly becomes conformed to the thinking of the world and adopts the wrong criteria.

The substance of Chapters 5–8 was contained in a series of Epilogues on television, which I gave in 1964 sponsored by Rediffusion.

Unless otherwise noted, quotations from the Bible are from the Revised Standard Version.

✠ GRAHAM WILLESDEN

Feast of St. James the Great
1970

CHAPTER I

THE Christian life is a gift of God, but that is not what most people think. The popular view, shared, it must be confessed, by many people in the Church, is that the Christian life is something which man does to help him to be a better person. A very common answer to the question, 'What is a Christian?' is 'Someone who is trying to live in accordance with the teaching of Jesus Christ'.

The gift of God is eternal life. That is the Gospel of the New Testament. God gives to man a new relationship to Himself. It is a relationship which is to be lived out in this life but which will abide for ever. It is a relationship made possible by the Life, Passion, Death and Resurrection of Jesus Christ, who is alive for evermore.

The whole of the New Testament shows that the purpose for which Christ lived, died and rose again is not to reveal a new morality or provide a new way of helping men to discover God. Christ is the first of a new race. In Him men and women can become new creatures. In Him, God offers to man something which he did not have before and which he cannot obtain by his own efforts. Saint John sums it up when he writes, 'Herein is our love, not that we loved God but that he loved us'. At the heart of the Christian Gospel is the fact that God has taken the initiative and reconciled us to Himself in Christ, not because of anything we have done to deserve it but from His love for us.

Having received the gift of our new relationship to God, we are then enabled to become the kind of people God wants us to be, which also means truly becoming ourselves. We are enabled to show those qualities of life and character which are the result of that relationship. Christian virtues are the fruit of our fellowship with God in Christ. They are not the means by which we achieve it.

When Saint Paul is writing to Christians and trying to help them to behave in a more Christian way, he almost invariably begins by reminding them of what God has done and of what it means for them. Then he uses some such phrase as 'for this cause' and draws out the implications for them in the way they should behave. 'God, rich in mercy, for the great love he bore us, brought to life in Christ . . . I entreat you then; . . . as God has called you, live up to your calling' (Eph. 2 : 5 and 4 : 1).

Becoming a Christian is not something which is limited to those with a particular temperament, or with certain intellectual qualities. The Gospel is for everyone. To become a Christian means acceptance of our dependence upon God and being willing to receive a gift from Him. It is for this reason that, as we shall see, God provides a simple way in which the gift is imparted—baptism—which is the same for every man or woman.

Once we have received the new relationship to God in Christ then we discover what God requires of us in response to this love; not because He is hard and demanding but because He knows what we are really capable of becoming. We learn that in Christ every part of our being is to be fulfilled. It is a slow process with ups and downs because God respects the free-will which He has given us and wants a willing response. But as we come to see His purpose for us and what we are in Christ, we learn for ourselves that to serve Him is to be truly free—free to become what we know we can be by the grace of God.

CHAPTER II

THE context in which the New Testament, indeed the Bible as a whole, makes sense is given to us in the Prologue to the Bible, the early chapters of Genesis. There, in dramatic picture language, the situation in which man finds himself is described. Created by God to live in fellowship with God, man refuses to accept his creatureliness, his dependence upon God, and becomes alienated from Him. Man's alienation from God results in his alienation from his fellow men and in conflict within himself. 'The good that I would I do not and the evil that I would not that I do.'

It is this situation which leads man to try to justify himself and his existence. The preacher who uses the word 'justification' to-day is likely to be accused of being irrelevant and of using unintelligible language. But, use the verb 'justify' rather than the noun, and it becomes clear that he is speaking about something with which the great majority of people are desperately concerned. Individuals, nations, groups within nations are all concerned to justify their existence. The pressure to do so becomes more acute as the problems of the world increase and the sense of insecurity and pointlessness becomes more oppressive.

Individuals seek to justify their existence by seeking status, both in terms of jobs which are recognised socially as desirable and in terms of financial reward. Nations seek to justify their existence by membership of treaty organisations, by space programmes or trade. Groups seek to justify themselves by protest. Sometimes it is a protest against real social injustice but not necessarily so. This becomes clear when, after some relief of the injustice is offered, the protest continues. The relief may be rejected because it represents the wrong kind of dependence on others. It may also perpetuate or even intensify the insecurity against which the protest is being made.

The Christian Gospel does not deny that it is right for a

man to seek to be justified. The desire to be recognised as a person with a purpose to be achieved is a natural and proper characteristic of human beings. In the parable of the Pharisee and the Publican our Lord recognised the need for a man to be justified. What He condemned was the attempt of the Pharisee to justify himself. The justifying of the Publican was a gift of God.

At the heart of the Gospel lies the fact of man's acceptance by God. Man is justified by God when he accepts that his only real status and any purpose for his life lies in his relationship with God and comes to receive the gift of that relationship with God. In Christ man is given the status of a son of God. He is given a new existence and a new relationship which he then implements in his worship and prayer and is expressed in his behaviour. He does not worship, pray and try to live respectably in the hope that as a result he will, by his own efforts, win a new relationship with God. Such may be what the world thinks Christians are trying to do but it is not the way of the Gospel.

CHAPTER III

TO accept that I need a new relationship with God means accepting that my present relationship is not the right one. It is for this reason that faith is the opposite of sin. Faith is the expression of our willingness to accept our dependence upon God. Christian faith recognises and accepts that we are powerless to do so by ourselves but that God has taken the initiative to make it possible. Penitence is not simply the expression of sorrow for our impotence, for, if it is truly impotence which we share with all mankind, it is a state in which we find ourselves and for which we are not responsible. We may regret it deeply but we cannot be penitent for it. Penitence starts with sorrow for our condition and for our willingness to let it continue but goes on to recognise that we cannot extricate ourselves from it unaided. Penitence embodies both the recognition that we do not live in the right relationship to God and our inability to achieve it.

The New Testament word for penitence means change of heart. It is not merely an attitude of regret. It reflects the willingness for something to be done about our condition. It recognises that only God can do this. The element of sorrow is present because, at this stage, we have a glimmering of what God wills for us as human beings and see ourselves in relation to Him.

It is at this point that penitence passes into faith—the acceptance that God has in Christ reconciled us to Himself and will give us the new relationship to Him. We do not rely upon our faith to save us or to recreate us. It is our faith which brings us to accept the healing, reconciling, re-creating word of our Lord.

While, as we shall see, we come in a moment of time in a particular act to be accepted by God, we have also to live by faith. We live in a continuing and deepening state of dependence upon God as we live in Christ, which liberates us. As a result we learn to love and obey God generously and spontaneously in the glorious liberty of the sons of God.

Christians live perpetually under both the love and mercy of God. By His love, we are enabled to be grasped more and more by the revelation of Himself which He has given in Christ. Our faith, which initially may be a simple trust in our Lord, is given content and we perceive more and more its implications for our lives. By His mercy we are enabled to see more and more what God calls us to be and how far short we fall. We come to see both the cost of God's forgiveness as we live under the Cross, and its depth, as we become aware of the holiness of life to which we are called. So our faith and our penitence are renewed. We bring forth the fruit of joy, one of the hall-marks of the Christian life.

CHAPTER IV

THE word 'faith' is, of course, also used to express the content of Christian belief. It is for this reason that some suppose that it is our intellectual belief or assent which justifies our calling ourselves Christians. Were that the case, we should be restricting both the revelation which God gives to us of Himself and His loving action towards us by our ability to comprehend it. The Gospel would not be for everyone—only for those with a certain intellectual capacity. Many would be excluded from Christian discipleship: some, because they lacked the necessary mental equipment, and others because they could not assent to this or that article of belief or the way in which it was expressed. The Gospel is for everyone but that does not mean that the intellectual aspect of the Christian life is unimportant and to be minimised. To live as a Christian we must be prepared for every aspect of our being to be stretched to the fullest extent. God gave us our minds and they are to be used in His service.

The use of our minds must not, however, be isolated from the rest of our Christian life. Thinking about the truth as revealed in Christ must take place in the context of our worship, our prayer and our life in the worshipping community. It must also be part of our life of obedience. We must learn to live under the truth as revealed in scripture, worship and prayer. Faced with something in the belief of the Church which we find it difficult to accept or understand, our question must be 'What is God wanting to tell me about Himself in this?' not 'Can I swallow this whole?'. It is, of course, the duty of those who have to teach and preach in the Church to stand under the judgment and the mercy of God, so that they communicate what is of God and not simply what is of themselves.

In the exercise of our minds as Christians we must constantly remind ourselves that people differ in their ways of thinking and in the extent to which they have responded to the love of God. What may seem very crude or unsophisticated to one person may to another convey the very essence of some aspect of Christian truth. What may be luminously clear to a person of real holiness may be a stumbling block to someone who has a long way to go in the Christian life. It may possibly be a stumbling block for the very purpose of making him face the demands of Christian discipleship.

Just as people differ, so do their temptations. Some face recurrent temptations to anger and to misuse of authority; others temptations to lust or sloth. But others face the temptation so to hedge what they say about the belief of the Church with a thousand qualifications that the simple but utterly demanding message of the Gospel is blurred. This is a temptation to which those of us who are called to be pastors of the flock are particularly prone. While we must seek to understand the difficulties of others and help them to work out the intellectual implications of Christian faith, we must not project our difficulties upon them and create problems for them. Our Lord was not afraid to speak of the demands of God in simple and uncompromising terms, though He was willing to answer questions and deal with difficulties which the disciples raised. If we, both priests and laymen, do not follow His example in proclaiming the Gospel, the hungry sheep will look up and not be fed.

CHAPTER V

MANY people find it difficult to believe that the meaning of life and the meaning of human history hinge upon events which took place a very long time ago. Wise men, they say, and holy men have argued and meditated throughout the centuries both before and after the birth of our Lord about the answer to the question, 'What are we here for?' Is the answer really to be found in something quite as simple and ordinary as the birth of one Baby? Is the answer to be found in His untimely death at the age of thirty-three?

We may find it disconcerting that such should be the case, but it should not surprise us. Although ideas—what people think—matter a great deal, history is made up of things that actually happened. It is what we do with our ideas that affects the lives of people. History is not a continuous flow of ideas; it is a succession of events, some more important, some less, some remembered, some forgotten. The quickest act, occupying but a short space of time, can have unimagined results. Good ideas are not much use to a drowning man, but the stretching out of a hand can save him. God has not just told us how to live. He has come to share the conditions of our human existence with us. He chose to enter into a new relationship with His created world and with the people who live in it, and to do so in a way which is effective for all time. The Incarnation is the supreme instance of the fact that God chooses to use the particular to achieve a universal purpose. At the beginning of the Biblical history He calls one man, Abraham, to be the father of one people, through whom He prepares the world for the coming of the Christ. Throughout the history of that people He uses particular men, places and things, as the means of that preparation. They were told, for example, to offer sacrifice in certain places with certain things through certain people. One of the functions of the prophets was constantly to remind them that they did so in order that they might learn to live a sacrificial life offering themselves, and their possessions, in thankful obedience to God and that the particular acts were not a substitute for this.

Then, at the turning point of human history, man is re-created in the one Person, Jesus the Christ, who, as Man, does for man what man could not do for himself. The new life thus made available is then communicated to mankind through the Church. It is through a particular act—Baptism—that men and women are made both members of the Church and new creatures in Christ. It is through a particular act—the Eucharist—that Christ perpetually renews and sustains His Church.

The trouble is that we do not like the concrete, the specific, the definite, especially where religion is concerned (which is, of course, everywhere). The concrete demands a response. We prefer pious generalities, vague hopes and exhortations, which enable us to say, 'Well, that is a very interesting point of view', and remain uncommitted. But God does not. He takes a human body and human nature. Our Lord died upon an actual cross at a moment of time. He rose from the dead on the first Sunday morning, His body having been laid in a tomb with a solid stone over the entrance. He told His Church to do something using bread and wine as the means of understanding and sharing what He had done. We may not like the fact of Bethlehem and Calvary, but we cannot escape them. Men reject them and parody them, but they cannot ignore them. Even after nearly two thousand years, books are still written seeking to prove that the story of Bethlehem is a myth and that our Lord did not really die but was resuscitated. The Eucharist still provokes the question, 'How can this man give us His flesh to eat?', which men asked when our Lord spoke of Himself as the Bread of Life.

Nevertheless, it is the fact that God works through the specific and the concrete which makes the Gospel available for everyone. 'Repent and be baptised' was the conclusion of Saint Peter's sermon in the Acts of the Apostles. To pass through the waters of baptism is the same for all, of whatever temperament, ability, intelligence or age. All receive the same when we stretch out to be given the Sacrament of the Body of the Lord, though each receives according to his need. Such is the generosity and mercy of God who wills that all men should have the fullness of life in Christ.

CHAPTER VI

MOST people have at one time or other had the agonising experience of standing beside someone who is enduring great grief or who is racked by physical pain and feeling utterly powerless to help. The stock phrases, however deeply we may feel them, seem wholly inadequate—'I am so sorry, I do sympathise'. We ask pathetically if there is anything we can do.

What we really want to do is to be able to share the experience of the person whom we love and for whom we are concerned while in every way remaining ourselves. We want to be able to take part of their grief or pain upon ourselves. We want to identify ourselves with them, yet remain wholly ourselves.

This deep instinct of man when faced with someone else in agony of mind or body leads to an understanding of what happened in Bethlehem. God Himself, while remaining in every way God and still sustaining the Universe at every point, identified Himself with us. He took our human nature and a human body and lived our human life with us and for us.

The Church has always had to fight for the truth that Jesus is both God and man. In one of the Creeds (which were the result of the efforts to maintain this truth), we say, Sunday by Sunday, that we believe our Lord to be God of God, Light of Light, Very God of Very God, Begotten not made, being of one substance with the Father, by whom all things were made.

What we are saying in those words, which come like repeated blows of a hammer, is that our Lord was not a creature, someone made by God, He was God Himself acting in human history.

When we talk about God, we say that He is Personal—we say, in fact, that He is Three Persons in one God. We speak of Him as Personal because it is the highest description of a living being we can use. We mean that He wills, that He loves, that He cares. He is the source of all free will, of all love, of all compassion. We do not imagine that our words are adequate. What we are really saying is that God is not just an abstract, changeless, impersonal principle. He has created man with free will, able to choose and He willed to share with man the results of disobedience so that man could be enabled to choose aright and to live in all the glory of a proper human being.

It is important that we hold fast to the truth that our Lord is God because, if it were not true, we could not go on believing that God is love. We would admire and reverence the wonderful life of the Man Jesus but we would not be reconciled to God. Jesus would stand before us as the victim of an unyielding and unfriendly God who demanded that such a man should live and die. Easter would be no longer the glorious demonstration of the ultimate victory of Love. It would become a demonstration by man that he could conquer in spite of the way in which God had made him.

It is important because also it shows that God is 'He who is', existing in His own perfect Being, independent of space and time *and* that He is the source of all Being, of all Life, of Love in the Universe which He has made. In other words, it shows us that the world is God's world and all that happens in it is God's concern. The Incarnation—that is the term we use to describe what God the Son did and its significance—has been called a rescue operation. Yes, it was a rescue operation, but not to salvage a few bits and pieces from a wreckage. God became Man to enable man to deal with the situation in which he finds himself but He also became Man to show us what He really intended man and the Universe to be. We Christians tend to concentrate too much upon the rescue and not enough upon the new vision of man which our Lord gives us and which He makes it possible for us to achieve.

Many people, if they talk about our Lord being truly Man, concentrate upon the fact that He really shared all the *difficulties* of human existence. He was hungry. He was thirsty. He was tempted. He was misunderstood, scorned and ridiculed. He was forsaken by His friends. Finally, He suffered an agonising death by crucifixion.

All this is perfectly true and we need to be reminded of it. Our Lord really did suffer as a man suffers. But He did not become Man simply in order to suffer. His suffering was necessary because of what He came to do.

An early Christian saint, Irenaeus, who was Bishop of Lyons and lived from about A.D. 130–200, described this quite simply, 'Because of His boundless love', says Irenaeus, 'He became what we are in order that He might make us what He is'. Our Lord became Man in order to bring about an entirely new relationship between God and Man.

CHAPTER VII

OUR LORD came to remedy our situation. He came to live our human life as God intended it to be lived. But His obedience to God was not simply that of a servant to his master. He came to live a life of willing obedience freely given out of love and in trust, as a son trusts and obeys his father. He came to create a new relationship with God by which our human life would be perfected, transformed and given a new meaning.

This obedience He had to live out in the face of sin and evil. He had to show how, if a man really trusted God, he would be transformed, not destroyed. So our Lord took all that the powers of evil could bring to bear upon Him. Ultimately when they had done all that they could to break Him, He accepted the last attack, that of physical death. But our Lord died, committing His whole cause into the Father's hands. At no point could evil get any response from Him. He lived a truly human life in perfect friendship with the Father in the face of all that the powers of evil could do to destroy it by trying to get Him to distrust God.

Our Lord rose on the third day. Death could not hold Him. He rose, still Man—the first of a new race of men. For He lived His life, died and rose again that men might share what He had done.

'As in Adam all die, even so in Christ shall all be made alive.' Saint Paul, who wrote these words, saw our Lord not merely as the beginning of a new race but also as its fulfilment. It is the hidden purpose of God made known in Christ that 'the Universe, all in heaven and on earth, might be brought into a unity in Christ'. The disintegration which man brings about left to himself is to be replaced by the bringing of all people and things together in harmony in Christ. So we are to attain, says Saint Paul, to 'our full manhood measured by nothing less than the full stature of Christ'.

When, by birth from a human mother, God the Son who is the Creator of Man becomes Man, He re-creates and restores the human race and with it the whole of Creation. Man, as he responds to what God has done in Christ, is enabled to fulfil the purpose for which he was made. Left to ourselves we become the centre of warring factions, with no single over-ruling purpose in our life, each part of us seeks to control the whole. In Christ, we can learn to allow each aspect of our nature to express itself fully and wholly taking its place with one single directed Godward action. This action includes our bodies, and it includes the whole of the physical creation with which we are part. We are enabled to see creation and use it so that the glory of the God who made it is revealed and the resources of the universe are made available for all men.

CHAPTER VIII

THE story of the Ascension of our Lord, as recounted in Scripture, is a very simple one. He had appeared to His disciples in ways which made it clear that He had risen in the whole of His humanity. He had not left His body behind, as of no account, or beyond the scope of the divine power. He, the Word, by whom all things were made, had taken His creation through death and had risen, mind, body and spirit.

At His Ascension, He leaves them in His body, as He had done before, but now evidently for the last time. The manner of His departure also made it clear that He was entering upon a new mode of existence and activity. No longer would they look for Him, here or there. The cloud was the sign of the eternal presence of God, and the Lord, both God and Man, is to be with them everywhere and at all times. Vindicated in the Resurrection, He now quietly receives the glory which He had before the world began. The New Testament draws out elsewhere the significance of the act. The Ascended Christ is proclaimed King of Creation which He had redeemed. Through His death, wherein He defeated evil, all things are brought under His sovereign power.

The Ascended Christ is the Forerunner. He is the firstborn of many brethren. In Him human nature fulfils the purpose for which it was created—union with God. Man is seen to be able to live with God and not die. The Ascended Christ is the Eternal Priest, ever living to make intercession for us. Through His sacrificial death, we can receive forgiveness, and be reconciled to God. 'It makes us free to enter boldly into the sanctuary by the new, living way which he has opened for us through the curtain, the way of his flesh' (Heb. 10 : 19, N.E.B.).

He who accepts what Christ has done comes to pledge his allegiance to Christ the King. No longer does he speak simply of Jesus or Jesus the Christ but speaks of Him as Lord, numbered among the company of those whom God has 'rescued from the domain of darkness and brought us away into the kingdom of his dear Son' (Col. 1 : 13, N.E.B.). He is liberated to live as one who has been reconciled and united to God in Christ. Here and now in the circumstances of the life and not in spite of it, he is enabled to live in fellowship with the living God, a fellowship which is eternal and extends beyond the grave. He has to save the world in the name and power of Christ, that the world may be brought into obedience to the living God in His glory.

CHAPTER IX

THE Resurrection is the standing evidence that he who puts his trust in God is not confounded. The Ascension proclaims that the risen Lord is not only alive but present eternally as Christ the King.

The New Testament also makes it clear that both Resurrection and Ascension enable man to live in a new relationship to God. It also speaks insistently of the relationship between the individual Christian and the risen Christ. Christians are presented not merely as those who try and follow the risen Christ, but as those who have actually been incorporated into Him and made sharers of His risen life.

The starting point of the Christian life is what God has done in Christ. This, however, includes both the actions of Christ in His Life, Death and Resurrection and the action by which God has incorporated men and women into Christ. So, Saint Paul, in his letters, follows a pattern of thought in which he begins with praise for the redeeming work of Christ, then refers to what Christians are by God's action as a result of that redeeming work and only then speaks of the kind of behaviour which a Christian should exhibit. For him, the way a Christian lives is the working out of the implications of what God has done for us and of what He has made us. 'He destined us in love to be his sons through Jesus Christ according to the purpose of his will to the praise of his glorious grace which he freely bestowed on us in the Beloved. In him we have a redemption through his blood, the forgiveness of our trespasses according to the riches of his grace which he lavished upon us. . . . I, therefore, a prisoner for the Lord, beg you to lead a life worthy of the calling to which you have been called' (Eph. 1 : 7 and 4 : 1).

If, then, the Christian way of life is the gift of God, how do we receive it? The New Testament gives us a double answer, which we must not try and separate. Faith and the Sacrament of Baptism is the answer. Faith in this sense is the willingness to accept our dependence upon God and to accept that in Christ God enables us to love and serve Him. We come with that willingness to Baptism to be the object of God's love and to receive the benefits of the Death and Resurrection of Christ. We do not rely upon our faith to save us. It is our faith which brings us to accept the healing, reconciling work of Christ which we experience in the Sacraments which He has ordained. The Sacrament of Baptism is not given to us to help us to find God. It is given to us as an act through which our Lord has promised to receive those who come accepting what He has done for mankind. 'In the Sacraments the Church in obedience, faith and humility acts in reliance upon our Lord's promise and power, not presumptuously but confident that He will not fail us.' [1] Our faith brings us to be incorporated *by God* in Baptism into the company of faithful people, which is the Body of Christ. So it is that as Professor Mackinnon has said of the ordinary Christian: 'His hope is grounded on what he *is*, a member of Christ, repossessed by God because baptised into Christ's death.' [2]

[1] *Growing into Union,* C. O. Buchanan, E. L. Mascall, J. I. Packer, the Bishop of Willesden, S.P.C.K. 1970, p. 61.

[2] *The Church of God,* Dacre Press 1940, p. 78.

CHAPTER X

HAVING been incorporated into Christ in Baptism, the Christian finds himself a member of a community. No one can be a Christian by himself, for in being united into Christ, he is also united to other Christians. The Church to which he now belongs is unlike any other body. The greater part of it is already in the world to come. The newly-baptised Christian is a member of the Holy Communion which includes our Lady, the Apostles, Evangelists and Martyrs. This he may frequently find it hard to remember as he takes his place in the local congregation. Screwtape, writing to his nephew and junior devil, Wormwood, says: 'One of our allies at present is the Church itself. Do not misunderstand me. I do not mean the Church as we see her spread out through all time and space and rooted in eternity, terrible as an array with banners. That, I confess, is a spectacle which makes our boldest tempters uneasy. But fortunately it is quite invisible to these humans. All your patient sees is the half-finished, sham-Gothic creation on the new housing estate.' So Wormwood is bidden to make the new Christian's mind 'flit to and fro between an expression like "the body of Christ" and the actual faces in the next pew.' [1]

This situation should not surprise us and for two reasons. First, because each of us knows that if the Church on earth claimed to be perfect, there would be no room for us in it. As soon as we joined it, it would cease to be perfect. We know that what has happened to us is not the result of what we have done. We know that we were accepted in Christ in our baptism not because of our merit, but because of our need. We know that it is by the living act of God that we have been forgiven and set in a new relationship to God. We also know that we have to 'walk worthy of our vocation' and live out the implications of what God has done for us.

Secondly, the New Testament leads us to expect it. At one

[1] *The Screwtape Letters,* C. S. Lewis, Bles 1942, pp. 15–16.

and the same time Saint Paul can address the Christians to whom he writes as members of Christ, brothers in faith, God's people, those whose life lies hidden with Christ in God, and tell them to lay aside all anger, passion, malice, cursing and filthy talk.

Saint Peter describes his readers as having been made members of a chosen race, a royal priesthood, a dedicated nation, but he also speaks very realistically about the temptations to which they will be subjected.

The contrast springs from the very nature of the Gospel. God accepts us as we are and sets us in a new creative relationship to Himself, in which we are set free to respond to what He has done. The Church on earth will, therefore, always be a very 'mixed' society. It will, at any given moment, contain those who have responded generously to the love of God and are allowing Him to transform them into the likeness of Christ, though even such people will have their imperfections, weaknesses and lapses, this side of the grave. It will also contain those who have only just been incorporated into Christ, as they are, with their old sins and habits, which will take a good deal of eradication. If the Church of God here on earth has not room for both it will have ceased to be true to its nature and will have substituted 'another Gospel' for the true Gospel of acceptance by the grace of God.

CHAPTER XI

THE newly-baptised Christian can rightly expect to find himself in a strangely exciting community. It should be a community of people who are extraordinarily joyful but who are very realistic about themselves and the world in which they live. It should be a company of people who are joyful because they know what they are by God's love and live daily under His mercy. It should be a company of people who live in a creative way in obedience to the Holy Spirit, yet who are both set free and disciplined to live creatively by constant reference to the Cross, Resurrection and Ascension of Christ. It should be a company of those who are learning to live together in love because they know they are loved by God and who are continually helping each other to grow in responsc to that love. It should be a community of people in which, as nowhere else, they should be accepted as they are, persons in their own rights with talents and temperaments which they can by grace consecrate for God, without being forced into a single mould. It should be a community of people who are aware of the world in which they live, and go out from their life in community with sensitivity, courage and faith, to bring the love of God to the world.

All this the newly-baptised has a right to expect from the descriptions of the Church in the New Testament. He will probably be prepared for the fact that the world will have some strange ideas both about the Church to which he now belongs and to his newly-professed Christian faith. His non-Christian friends will make him aware that in his beliefs and practices and the world-outlook which now possesses him, he is swimming against the tide. Whatever he may say, they will almost certainly think that he is setting himself up as better than they are. They will certainly wonder why on earth he wants to spend his Sunday mornings in Church instead of lying in bed reading the papers or going to the seaside, if it is a fine day.

What he may not be prepared for is what he will find in the Church. One Christian said about a year later to the bishop who baptised and confirmed him: 'I knew there would be people like me who aren't very good, but what I've found so difficult is that everyone seems to be concerned about things like the choir or running the Stewardship Campaign. No one seems to talk about the things I thought really mattered—like worship and prayer and forgiving people. The Vicar has tried to get me to go on the P.C.C. but he hasn't asked about my prayers.' No one who has experienced the life of the Church of England from within will say that he was talking about an imaginary situation. It is all too true. To face the facts should not depress us. Rather it should bring us back to our dependence upon God, and make us ask what should mark the life of a Christian.

CHAPTER XII

IF the Gospel is for everyone and if the Church is the community in which people are to be enabled to live in accordance with the Gospel, then what is required of the ordinary Christian must be possible for everyone and not for a select few. Too often, at the present day, the impression is given that the 'real' Christian, the committed Churchman, is the person who is fully involved in the mechanics of keeping the Church going as an institution. This is to be deplored for two reasons. First because it means that the real purpose of the Church's life has been lost sight of. The Church exists to proclaim and extend the Kingdom of God by His grace. It is the duty and privilege of every Christian to take part in this work. The maintenance of the Church as an institution is the means by which the Church is enabled to carry out its primary work. The internal life and organisation of the Church must be judged by whether it serves this end. It must never become an end in itself. Grateful though we should be to those who look after accounts and buildings, sit on committees and go to conferences, we must never imagine that they are doing 'Church work', and that it is simply the duty of the ordinary Christian to back them up. It is the ordinary Christian who should be doing the Church's work and the job of the few who can be engaged in the domestic affairs of the Church is to enable him to do it better. The second reason why such an allocation is deplorable is because it limits and undermines the Gospel. If the 'real' Christian is the person who has the time or money to be able to take part in such activities, then the Gospel is not for everyone. The majority of Christians are very heavily committed in their ordinary lives which, rightly, have first priority. The demands of a large family or of aged relations may result in a mother having very little spare time. The unmarried man or woman who has to do a full-time job, which may involve weary hours of travel, do the shopping, and keep the house in order unaided, finds it very difficult to become regularly committed to outside engagements. All too often those who, having heavy commitments at home, might properly look for help from other members of the congregation, are expected to go to this meeting, attend that conference or organise that activity. In too many parishes the impression is given that the basic Christian duties of worship, prayer, bible study and witness in one's job are not enough. But it is only when Christians are faithful to these activities that they are rooted in the Cross and Resurrection and enabled by God to respond to His love and manifest the fruits of Christian discipleship.

CHAPTER XIII

WHAT then should be expected of the average Christian if he is to be regarded as committed in his response to God and in his discipleship? It is important to distinguish between what he does as the continued expression of his response to God and the qualities which he shows in his life as a result of the deepening of that response. A Christian is committed to worship and, in particular, to take his place regularly as the People of God meet to obey the Lord's command by celebrating the Holy Communion. In so doing, he renews his intention of living for God in response to the love of God. He proclaims with the Church his dependence upon the Passion, Resurrection and Ascension of our Lord. He is renewed in his union with the Living God. He proclaims his membership of the Body of Christ and his willingness to learn to die to his self-centredness to live as a member of the Holy Communion. He commits himself afresh to share in the mission of the Church as he lives in the world.

Secondly, a Christian is committed to pray as the personal expression of the fellowship with God in Christ which he has received. By his progress, he learns to live in communion with God in and through this world.

Thirdly, a Christian is committed to read and study the Scriptures and to learn in obedience to be grasped by the truths which God reveals to us in Christ about Himself. He will do this in the way which is appropriate for his own mind and intelligence. But do it he must. Too many Christians have full hearts and empty minds.

It is by worship, prayer and meditation upon Scripture that the Christian is brought to the 'flesh and blood' of Jesus as Sir Edwyn Hoskyns used to put it, that is, to the events of the Gospel by which his vision of God's purpose is renewed and his own response disciplined and strengthened. He is also renewed in his union with the Living Christ and enabled both to see what this demands and to put these demands into effect.

As a result, he is enabled to grow as a Christian and produce the qualities which should mark his life as a Christian. But this will only happen if he sees his worship, his prayer and his meditation on Scripture in the light of the Gospel—that is, if he worship, prays and reads Scripture in a spirit of dependence upon God. He must constantly remember that, as Saint John puts it: 'Herein is our love not that we loved God but that he loved us'. He must also be prepared for the fact that if he does these things in this spirit, strange things will happen to him. He will find that his judgments and his priorities will change. He will find himself constrained to do things in love and compassion which he would not have contemplated doing before. What will probably surprise him even more is that as this happens, he will discover that he is becoming more himself.

CHAPTER XIV

AT the heart of the life of the Church and as its central act of worship stands the Holy Communion, the Eucharist, the Lord's Supper as it is variously called. To take part in the Eucharist is the characteristic act of the Christian. In the Breaking of the Bread—another Scriptural title for this service—the Church proclaims its dependence upon what God has done in the Passion, Death, Resurrection and Ascension of Christ and is sustained and strengthened in its life as the community which was brought into being by these events.

It is an act which reflects the very nature of the Church. This is clear if we think for a moment of why we come to take part. We come because of what God has done for us and because of what we are by grace. We come because we are those who have been translated into the Kingdom of Christ and who have pledged our allegiance to Christ the King.

We do not come because we think we are good enough. We do not come because we think that it is a way of earning merit with God so that He will condescend to accept us. We do not come because we find it a helpful or inspiring service. We come because we are and know ourselves to be the objects of God's love—'. . . accepted in the Beloved'—and bold to say: 'Our Father' because we can say it with our Lord.

We come relying not upon ourselves but upon the promise and power of God. That is what we mean when we speak of the Eucharist as a Sacrament. Taking part in the Eucharist represents our response to the Covenant which God has made with us. We come recognising what we are by the grace of God, proclaiming our acceptance of it and rejoicing in it. In this sense, the Eucharist is the characteristic act of our glory.

But we also come knowing that whilst we are indeed the sons of God, 'it does not yet appear what we shall be'. We have a long way to go to implement in our lives the significance of what God has done for us. So the Lord gives us Himself in the Sacrament of His Body and Blood that we may be more truly His members and transformed into His likeness.

In the Eucharist God has given to us an act which corresponds with the reality of our situation. In it we give thanks for what we are and for His acceptance of us in Christ. By taking part in the act we also express our willingness to become in His hands what He wants us to be. As the Christian comes through the Church door on a Sunday morning, he is, in effect, saying: 'Lord, you have made me Your own. You have accepted me as I am to be a member of Your people, the royal priesthood. I come in clothed with the glory of Christ to worship You and to praise You on behalf of all creation.' But at one and the same time he is saying: 'Lord, have mercy. I have not lived as one who is Your son. I am not yet what You want me to be. I do not yet know the depths of Your love or the splendour of Your truth. But I come because You have accepted me even as I am. I come trusting in Your love and forgiveness asking You to cleanse, love and renew me as Your son.'

CHAPTER XV

'THE Holy Communion' is both a title for the central and characteristic act of worship of the Christian Church and a description of the Church itself. In both senses the word 'holy' is only justified because holiness is the result of the calling and action of God.

The Breaking of the Bread is the Holy Communion, because the Church comes to obey the Lord's command, confident that He will not fail us. An ordinary meal can be, and should be, an expression of our thanksgiving and a means of communion with God. But when we come to eat *this* Bread and drink *this* Cup, we know that we proclaim the Lord's death till He come. We can say, with Saint Paul, 'the cup of blessing which we bless, is it not a participation in the blood of Christ? The bread which we break, is it not a participation in the body of Christ?' and say so, confidently expecting the answer 'yes'.

The mere sharing of bread and wine in a corporate act will not unite us to Christ nor to one another in Him. We are united to Christ and to one another when He takes the bread and says 'Take, eat, this is my Body' and 'Drink ye all of this: for this is the Blood of the new covenant', and we obey His command. The Holy Communion is not simply the 'sharing of the Bread and Wine' as the Series II Communion Service describes it. It is a sharing of the Bread and Wine, which by Christ's power and grace is the Communion of the Body and Blood of Christ. We are renewed in our union with our risen Lord and thereby renewed in our union with each other as members of His Body.

This we must remember as we seek to respond to the love of God and live in the way which is fitting to us as members of the Holy Communion. When the Church gathers together on a Sunday morning to make Eucharist, it is the meeting of those who have been 'accepted in the Beloved'. As we look at our neighbours in the pews we look at those whom the

Lord has also received into communion with Himself. As we come to receive the Sacrament of His Body and Blood we do not presume to come trusting in our own righteousness but in the manifold and great mercies of the Lord. There is no distinction in what we outwardly receive for we are all equally dependent upon the Lord. But He gives us of Himself in such measure and in such a way that each one individually can serve the Lord in his own particular way.

We see each other as those who have been 'accepted in the Beloved'; yes, but also as those who have been accepted as persons, each of whom has a unique contribution to make to the life of the whole Body. 'We are to grow up in every way into him who is the Head, into Christ, from whom the whole body, joined and knit together by every joint with which it is supplied, when each part is working properly, makes bodily growth and upholds itself in love' (Eph. 4 : 15–16).

Dependence on our Lord enables us to learn dependence on one another, recognising that others can supply what we cannot. Such dependence must not be of the servile kind which reduces a man to a mere pawn. It must be the dependence of openness in which we are prepared to receive as well as give, and which accepts our own imperfections and need to learn.

CHAPTER XVI

THE Christian comes to take part in the Eucharist because he has been baptized into Christ. He comes because having responded to the love of God he has been apprehended by God in Christ. 'Baptism', wrote Dietrich Bonhoeffer, 'is essentially passive—*being baptised, suffering* the call of Christ. In baptism man becomes Christ's one possession. . . . He is wrested from the dominion of the world and passes into the ownership of Christ.' [1] The Christian comes to the Eucharist because of what he has become in God's hands. It is because we are 'in Christ' that we can come. It is because we are 'in Christ' that we must come.

We must come because it is through the Eucharist that we are enabled to live out the meaning of our baptism. Saint Paul when writing to the Christians at Rome, asks if they have forgotten the meaning of their baptism. 'Have you forgotten that all of us who have been baptised into Christ Jesus were baptised into his death? We were buried therefore into him by baptism into death, so that as Christ was raised from the dead by the glory of the Father, we too might walk in newness of life' (Rom. 6 : 3–4). Our Lord suffered in His death the ultimate isolation which is the consequence of man's refusal of his dependence. Unbroken in His obedience to the Father, He is raised to be the first of the new race. Through His atoning and reconciling death, we are enabled to die to live—to die to our self-centred isolation and to live in union with Christ in His life-giving Body. Death to life *and* the corporate life are the complementary gifts of baptism. If we die to live it is to a life in the service of the People of God. We can only be members of Christ through dying to live.

So in the Eucharist, we come because of what we have become at God's hands. We come to show forth in the way which the Lord has given us, the source and means of our

[1] *The Cost of Discipleship,* revised edition, p. 206. Italics in original.

new life—His saving death. But we also come to receive the sacrament of His Body and Blood that we may by sharing in the redeeming power of His death be enabled to die daily and live as those who are in Christ.

In the Eucharist, the Christian community together proclaims its utter dependence upon the Cross of Christ from which it has its origin and the sovereignty of the risen Lord, Christ the King who is the Head of the community and who perpetually brings His Church to true discipleship. It does so after the manner of a sacrament. In other words it does so in a way which depends upon our Lord's promise and power and not upon the state of mind of those who worship. God provides the means of our proclamation so that in the very act of proclaiming our dependence upon Him, we may be delivered from dependence upon our own mood or feelings.

For participation in the Eucharist, no more and no less is required than for baptism; penitence and faith. We come with penitence for our acquiescence in our self-centredness and our willingness to live in isolation from God and one another. We come accepting what God has done for us in Christ. As the Gospel is for everyone, so also is baptism and so is the Eucharist. It is through our participation in the Holy Communion that our penitence is sharpened, our understanding of forgiveness is deepened and our faith is given content. So we are enabled to live out, both in our fellowship with God and one another, the dying to live of our baptism and to produce the fruit of Christian life.

CHAPTER XVII

IN prayer the Christian expresses the relationship to God which he has been given in Christ. It is, of course, natural for man to pray. Created by God and by his very existence witnessing to his dependence upon God, he is made in the image of God. He has both the gift of free will and the power of expressing the intention behind his actions. He should, therefore, offer to God his reasonable worship—the homage of an intelligent creature—by his willing and declared obedience to the will of God.

But all man's natural activities are spoilt by his self-sufficiency and disobedience. Prayer is no exception and, left to himself, man does not and cannot pray as he should. He forgets his dependence upon God, crying out only in moments of crisis. He refuses God his obedience yet still tries to pray.

In Christ, all man's natural activities are redeemed and raised to a new level. Again, prayer is no exception. Our Lord, in His earthly life, prayed as God intended man to pray. The Christian expressing in his prayers his relationship to God in Christ is to allow this prayer of Christ to be prayed in and through Him.

Our Lord in His own prayers, which expressed throughout His earthly life the perfect living homage of a son, addressed God as 'Father' and spoke of Him as 'My Father'. But He told His disciples to address God as 'Our Father'. He, the 'first-born among many brethren' tells us to come to the Father with Him. So we pray through Jesus Christ our Lord; in adoration 'Hallowed be Thy Name'; in obedience 'Thy kingdom come, Thy will be done'; in dependence 'Give us this day our daily bread'. It is through the Cross of Christ that we ask in penitence 'Forgive us our trespasses as we forgive those who trespass against us', and calling upon the power of the victorious Christ we pray 'Lead us not into temptation but deliver us from evil'. All Christian prayer is a sharing of Christ's prayer. Sometimes it is the corporate prayer of the Body of Christ gathered in one place. Sometimes it is the prayer of individual Christians as they live dispersed in the world. In corporate prayer, this Prayer of Christ is offered by the Church as His Body in its members, each member making his own contribution to the offering of the whole and learning, by taking part, what the Prayer of Christ means. In personal private prayer, the Christian learns how the Prayer of Christ is to be prayed in the particular circumstances of his own life. Each Christian will pray privately as he alone can pray. His prayer must become more and more in accord with the Prayer of Christ, but it will be expressed in the way which is individual to him.

As a unique member of the Body of Christ with a unique part to play in the offering of prayer made by the Church here on earth, he says: May the Prayer of Christ be prayed through me both as the expression of my own love of God and as the prayer of intercession for all among whom I live and for whom I must be concerned.

CHAPTER XVIII

HOW then should the Christian pray personally and privately? Can any general pattern of prayer be laid down? If each Christian must pray as he alone can pray, does not this rule out any general guidance on prayer which applies to everyone? It is important to distinguish between a pattern of praying and what we actually say—the content of our prayer. We need a pattern of prayer simply because we are human beings who live in space and time. We do not learn to pray at all times—to live our prayer—if we do not pray at set times. We do not learn to pray with the whole of our being unless we bring our bodies with our praying, presenting them a living sacrifice to God as well as offering our minds. We cannot try and behave as if we are angels, ignoring our bodies and space and time. If a man says that he loves his wife all the time and has, therefore, no need to give any special time to her for her own sake, we know what happens. His love withers and may die. He comes to take her for granted. So it is with our prayers. It is because we are concerned to love God at all times, to respond to Him with the whole of our being that we give time to Him.

Our Lord lived a life of prayer. Yet because He is human as well as divine, He gave time to prayer in His life whilst on earth. He withdrew for definite times of prayer. Sometimes we are told that He went to a lonely spot in the early morning before it was light. Sometimes He withdrew for prayer on a special occasion. Saint Luke tells us that before calling the Apostles He spent the night in prayer. In Gethsemane, He withdrew to pray before His betrayal and arrest. At other times our Lord prayed in the midst of activity. He prayed in His grief at the tomb of Lazarus. He prayed rejoicing in the Holy Spirit when the seventy-two disciples returned from their mission. He prayed during His Passion as the soldiers nailed Him to the Cross.

Whatever may be the circumstances of our personal life,

our private prayers should follow a pattern which includes these elements. First, there should be a morning offering of ourselves to God in response to His love, and an evening commendation when we commit ourselves into His hands. Secondly, there should be a regular element of withdrawal to be consciously in the presence of God for His sake. Thirdly, we should grow in the practice of praying to God in the midst of activity. The actual form of expression in which these three elements will be clothed will and must vary for each individual, as will also the time we spend upon them.

What we need to remember again and again is that all our prayer should be the expression of our relationship to God. We recollect that we are in Christ and do not pray to an unknown God or to a God whom we hope eventually to find. Our prayer is a response to the God who has already found us and who tells us to say: 'Our Father'.

CHAPTER XIX

IN the morning we offer ourselves and the day to God in response to His love. We give the intention to our work. It is for God, we say, and we ask Him to enable us to fulfil our intention. How long we spend upon this will depend partly upon our circumstances and partly upon our temperament. A young mother with several very young children will almost certainly be woken up by them; however early she may hope to get up. No one would expect her to leave them crying while she spends time in her morning offering. Yet she can, as she gets out of bed to attend to them, stop for a brief second and say, 'Lord, this day is for You; please help me to live it in the way You want'. Others with less urgent domestic circumstances yet with still a long list of things to do before going off for the day's work, can properly give time to stand or kneel in a conscious offering of themselves to God, recalling their vocation as Christians and expressing their dependence upon Him. Some will take part in the Eucharist which will for them be their morning offering. For most people, this will not be possible, unless they happen to be near a Church and also work nearby. Some will use a regular form of words, varying perhaps for each day of the week. Others called to a simple contemplative form of prayer will hold themselves silently and obediently before God in response to His love. What matters is whether the morning offering is made and whether it is made in the way which is right for the person who is making it. Then there is the evening commendation of ourselves into God's hands. Again, the form will vary. The unmarried daughter who works all day to support her aged mother, comes in to prepare the meal and probably to do some housework for which there may not be time before going to work next morning. That done, her mother expects her to sit up talking or reading to her and when she finally goes to bed, she is utterly worn-out. But even she can, as she falls into bed, pause to commit herself to God's care, with a prayer, perhaps silent, for forgiveness and renewal. Others will not have to wait until the last moment. I know of one man who says, 'Excuse me', at nine o'clock, and slips upstairs for his brief evening prayer because he does not want, as he puts it, '. . . to be dropping off when I speak to God'.

The simple pattern of morning and evening gives a rhythm to our life. It does more—it prepares us to cope with crises in a spirit of courage, hope and dependence upon Him. I was visiting an elderly woman in hospital who had just undergone a very serious operation of which the outcome was, humanly speaking, doubtful. She was still in pain when I spoke to her about her suffering. As she told me of the way in which she faced the operation, she said, 'As I was prepared for it, I just said, "Lord, here I am, Your servant"—and it was not difficult to say that, because I have been saying it every night of my life, as the last thing before I go to sleep'.

CHAPTER XX

DURING the day we should be acquiring the habit of expressing our relationship to our Lord in simple and direct prayer to Him. The very idea of 'habit' is frowned upon by some Christians to-day as being in some way contrary to the freedom which should mark the Christian life and as bringing in a mechanical element. In fact, acquiring a habit is an inevitable part of living as a human being. Our habits are the expression of the kind of person we are becoming and the means by which we grow in one direction or another. Our habits deliver us, for good or ill, from being at the beck and call of every whim or fancy that takes us. What matters is whether our habits are good or bad. To acquire Christian habits is part of that process which Saint Paul describes as not being conformed to the world, but being transformed by the renewing of our mind so we may prove what is the good, acceptable and perfect will of God.

Provided that we are being disciplined and nourished by our corporate worship and by our thinking over the Scripture, we need not shrink from speaking quite freely to our Lord. This we can and should do, to thank Him, to rejoice with Him, to praise Him, to ask for His help. When we see someone acting in compassion towards another, we can simply say, 'Thank You, Lord', to the Lord who is Love, and rejoice with Him. When we see an exquisite sunset or a beautiful flower, we can praise the Lord of all Creation. One difficulty for Christians is that we have let the world take what we ought to say. We are prevented from saying it aloud because we would be misunderstood. To say 'Christ!' should be a natural thing for Christians to say when they want to express their gratitude to the Lord of Creation. To say 'My God' should be a natural prayer for Christians for those involved when they read of a disaster or see an accident. The world says, unthinkingly perhaps, what we should be saying and in so doing reproaches us for our failure to relate all our activities to our Lord. We should be especially concerned to pray in this way when we anticipate difficulties or when we are doubtful if our discipleship will be strong enough to meet the demands upon it. We see someone coming along the road towards us. We find him trying and know that we are always provoked to say something which we regret afterwards. We can pray quite simply, 'Lord, here is So-and-So, and You know what happens when I meet him. Please help me this time to be more loving.' Or it may be that we may have to see someone, say in the course of business, who ridicules and attacks our faith. On the way, we should ask the Lord to give us wisdom and courage, and to help us to witness to Him and not to try and justify ourselves.

A good many Christians will pray about something beforehand but having done so, go from their prayer as if they were leaving the Lord behind. We should pray beforehand, certainly, but we must also remember that the occasion about which we have prayed takes place in the Presence of our Lord. Recollection of His Presence often checks us from the hasty or bitter word and sometimes shows us that our whole attitude needs a radical change.

This kind of prayer must not be a substitute for thinking about the implications of our Christian faith and discipleship. We have to wrestle with the problems of what is right and wrong in our behaviour and of what our priorities should be. We have to use our minds to the fullest extent of which we are capable. But our thinking must never be isolated. It must be part of our continuing relationship to God in Christ. Our thinking must be used and expressed in our prayer and also tested by it.

CHAPTER XXI

MANY Christians find that the greatest difficulty in prayer lies in finding or making time to be with God alone for His sake. As a result, some Christians question the necessity of doing so. Prayer must always be relevant, they say, and go on virtually to identify activity with prayer. I am praying when I am counselling someone, they will say, or when I am engaged in social action, and this is real prayer. Such an attitude both ignores the example and instructions of our Lord, and fails to recognise that for a human being the intention with which he does things is all important. I think it is very easy for 'intellectuals' to adopt this attitude without realising quite how their way of living differs from that of the majority of people. 'Intellectuals' are accustomed to ask the question 'Why?'—to reflect on the reasons for doing things and their ultimate significance and to do so as they go about their job, particularly as they carry out routine matters. But most people have to stop and pause to ask the question 'Why?' and need to be reminded to do so. When you stop your ordinary activities to pray you are, in fact, concerning yourself with the ultimate reason for all things—God Himself.

But why do Christians find it difficult to give time to God for His sake? The pressure and pace of life to-day are obvious reasons. So is the lack of privacy from which many people suffer both with regard to space and to the unwillingness of people to respect what others are doing and leave them undisturbed. Another reason lies in the fact that many Christians are not given clear enough advice about how to use such time.

I think there are more fundamental reasons. The first is that although we may underestimate the importance of prayer, the devil does not. He is quite happy for us to do other things because he knows that if he can keep us from praying, he can quickly corrupt the other things so that they serve his ends and not those of God. Thus he can succeed in turning our conviction into a harsh dogmatism which breeds lack of charity, our sincerity into a sentiment which avoids truth, and our compassion into condonation. He can succeed in getting us to the point where we think of God not in a spirit of adoration and obedience but in terms of His usefulness to man. The pressures not to pray are tremendous and they are not merely human.

Another fundamental reason is that to give time to God alone for His sake brings us face to face with God and His claims upon us. The mere giving of time is a recognition that we exist for Him. If you are a very busy person, it means accepting that you are not indispensable, and that for a space of time, you can leave your own affairs to give God your whole attention. It also means being prepared to accept unknown demands. To quote the devil Screwtape again, '. . . Once . . . a man trusts himself to the completely real, external invisible Presence, there with him in the room and hence knowable by him as he is known by it—when, then it is that the incalculable may occur. In avoiding this situation —this real nakedness of the soul in prayer—you will be helped by the fact that the humans themselves do not desire it as much as they suppose. There's such a thing as getting more than they bargained for! . . .' [1]

[1] *The Screwtape Letters,* C. S. Lewis, Bles 1942, p. 28.

CHAPTER XXII

WHEN and how should the average Christian go apart to pray? It is very difficult and even unwise to try and generalise. What matters is that Christians do spend some time alone with God for His sake. When they should do so depends very largely upon the circumstances of the individual. Some can and should do so at home. For others, this is virtually impossible and a church near the place of work will be the right place in which to pray during the lunch-hour or after work. This is not always easy, partly because so many churches are locked, and partly because if the church is open, too often people seem to be expected to do everything but pray. The problem of stealing from churches is serious, but churches could be kept open at least during the lunch-hour if enough Christians made it clear that they wanted to use them during that time. If a church can be kept open then people should be able to know when they can go to pray without being disturbed by such things as organ practice or cleaning. This will only happen if Christians insist that they want to use churches for prayer during the week. Some use the public library or an art gallery. Some who drive to work, draw up in a quiet place before returning home. Some get to church early and use the time before the service begins. Some should pray in this way, daily; some, weekly; some, twice a week; but what matters is that we give time to God for His sake.

How we spend the time again depends on the individual. Some will spend it reading Scripture and then quietly reflecting upon it, praying meanwhile and ending with a prayer. Others will do the same with some other book, for though Scripture is supreme and must not be neglected, we can learn from the experience of others who speak to our situation in their writings. Others will simply want to hold themselves in the Presence of God, directing their whole being towards Him in a simple act of adoration, penitence, love and thanksgiving, quietly turning back to Him again and again as distractions intervene. Some will spend the time saying the Lord's Prayer slowly, dwelling on each petition.

However we spend the time, we should say something like this when we come to begin our prayer, using, of course, our own words: 'Father, I have come apart, not to escape the world, but to be with You for Your sake. You have made me Your own. You have reconciled me to Yourself. But I find this hard to remember in the world. I so often think that everything depends on me and not on You. I find it hard to leave things in Your hands, even for this short time. Father, you have accepted me in Your Beloved Son, Christ, my Lord. In Him and through Him may I come to know You and be seized by Your Majesty, Power, Love, Compassion, Beauty and Holiness.'

It is as we learn to adore God for His sake in prayer that we find ourselves serving Him for His sake in the world, having been caught up by the Vision of His Splendour.

CHAPTER XXIII

MOST Christians seem to find it difficult to persist in regular reading of the Scriptures, though they recognise that it should be an integral part of their Christian discipleship. We will not spend time considering why this should be so, but rather consider ways which will help us to be more faithful.

There is no shortage of modern translations to-day. For private use, I think it is difficult to do better than use the Jerusalem Bible for the Old Testament and the translation by Prebendary J. B. Phillips for the New Testament. The latter, in particular, brings home in a very forceful way the fact that when Saint Paul was writing to the early Church, he was speaking to people like ourselves with the same spiritual problems. A few years ago, I was speaking to a Parochial Church Council which was sadly at sixes and sevens. In the course of my talk, I quoted from the twelfth chapter of Romans in Phillips' translation. Afterwards, a young man asked me what the splendid book was from which I had quoted, saying that it might have been written about them. He seemed very surprised to be told it was the New Testament.

Having got your modern translation, read it. Don't nibble at it, but read it so that you can appreciate the overall pattern and theme. Read one of Saint Paul's letters or a Gospel at a sitting. Don't spend your time reading books about the Bible until you have immersed yourself in it, though there is one book which really does help us to see how the Bible speaks to us about the fundamental issues of human life and our relationship to God. That is, *Reflections on the Psalms* by C. S. Lewis, which although primarily concerned with the Psalms, illuminates our understanding of the whole Bible. He helps us to do what Sir Edwyn Hoskyns tells us we must do. 'The Church does not require of us that we should master a new vocabulary but that we should apprehend the meaning of the commonest words in our language: it demands that we should not at the critical moment turn away from the meaning of words, but that we should wrestle with them and refuse to let them go. For from these common words, from "life" and "death", from "good" and "evil", from "judgment" and "mercy", there peers out at us from our quite normal, ordinary life, from the world of men and of things, a secret which concerns us and from which we cannot escape.'[1]

The secret is that life comes through death—death to our self-centredness by the power of the Cross, to a resurrection in Christ to new life in Him. At every point, Scripture in concrete historical ways forces us to face the issue. It is for this reason that our reading of Scripture must be set within the context of our worshipping life in the Church. The Word of the Lord which we hear in Scripture is sharper than any two-edged sword, and brings home to us the meaning of our baptism and of our participation in the Eucharist.

One of the best ways of reading Scripture is to take the Epistle or Gospel for the Sunday, and to read it in its context in the book from which it comes. Then we should ask the question 'To what must I die, and to what must I live as I come as one who has been baptised into Christ, to share in the communion of His Body and Blood?'

[1] *Cambridge Sermons*. The Language of the Church, S.P.C.K. 1938, p. 90.

CHAPTER XXIV

THE new life in Christ is a gift of God. But it is a gift which brings with it great demands. At first sight, this fact appears to conflict with the saying of our Lord that His yoke is easy and His burden light. It might also lead us to question the gift. If the gift brings demands, does it not savour of a bargain? Is not the Lord saying to us 'Come unto me all you who are weary and heavy laden', but demanding in return that we should meet His requirements? Put it that way the question seems to have some justification, but it does not accord with the Gospel.

God does not accept us as we are so that *in return* we may love and serve Him as a *quid pro quo*. He accepts in order that we may be liberated to serve the purpose for which we were created. Our difficulty in grasping this is twofold. In the first place, we do not have a sufficiently clear vision of God's purpose for us to see that it is the purpose for which we exist and is infinitely the best thing for us. It is for this reason among others, that a Christian worships, prays and meditates upon scripture. Thereby his vision of God is deepened and strengthened. We are enabled to see the will of God for what it is, 'good, acceptable and perfect'.

Secondly, we do not appreciate the nature of the gift. The gift of new life in Christ carries with it the gift of the ability to learn to obey the will of God generously and spontaneously. The new life in Christ enables us to become the kind of persons who will love the will of God and fulfil it. If we try to receive and live the new life in Christ while refusing our dependence upon God and continuing in our disobedience, then His demands indeed appear hard. Baptism involves dying to live through the power of Perfect Death to Life, that of our Lord.

The moral demands of the Christian life appear impossible in the light of self-interest, however carefully and wisely the various conflicting claims may have been judged. They have to be seen in the light of the Cross.

The Sermon on the Mount is often regarded as embodying the essential qualities of the Christian life. Rather it embodies the essential qualities of human life, which are made possible of realisation through the Cross. Taken in isolation, the Sermon on the Mount appears to present impossible and unattractive qualities. It is through the Cross that they become both possible and attainable. When we say 'through the Cross' we mean both through the unique offering of our Lord made thereon, and through the death to self-centredness and isolation and rising to a new life of obedience made possible for the Christian in Him.

As we now come to consider the qualities which a Christian must manifest in his life in the world, we shall look at the Beatitudes (St. Matt. 5 : 1–12) in the light of the Cross. It is by the quality of his life that the Christian primarily fulfils his responsibility to witness to the healing reconciling love of Christ.

CHAPTER XXV

'BLESSED are the poor in spirit, for theirs is the kingdom of heaven.' The Beatitudes are addressed to the disciples. 'Seeing the crowds, the Lord went up on the mountain, and when he had sat down his disciples came to him. And he opened his mouth and taught them saying'—What the Lord has to say is for those who have ears to hear. Although what He teaches them is true for everyman, its acceptance demands a radical change of heart.

The first quality of which our Lord speaks brings this home sharply. Those who are 'of the world' think in terms of possessions by which they may establish themselves. Our Lord speaks of poverty of spirit—that is of detachment—by which all that we are and all that we possess is seen as belonging to God and held in trust for Him.

Of such detachment our Lord is the perfect example. As Saint Paul says in his letter to the Church at Philippi, 'though he was in the form of God, did not count equality with God a thing to be grasped, but emptied himself, taking the form of a servant, being born in the likeness of men. And being found in human form he humbled himself and became obedient unto death, even death on a cross' (Phil. 2 : 6–8). He who is the eternal word, by whom all things were made: He who was in glory with the Father before the world was made, accepts a position of utter dependence upon the Father in our human life. He does not clutch that which is His by right. He accepts, as man, only that which the Father gives Him and rejects the temptation, which He suffers as man, to try and possess in His own right independently of the Father. 'The devil took him up to a very high mountain and showed him all the kingdoms of the world and the glory of them; and he said to him "All these I will give you if you fall down and worship me". Then Jesus said "Be gone Satan! for it is written, You shall worship the Lord your God and him only shall you serve".'

Saint Paul continues the passage quoted above with the words 'Therefore God has highly exalted him and bestowed on him the name that is above every name that at the name of Jesus every knee should bow, in heaven and on earth and under the earth and every tongue confess that Jesus Christ is Lord to the glory of God the Father'. The Lord, who as man renounced all things and committed Himself wholly to the Father, comes into His Kingdom. To be detached is not to despise the world or to seek to escape from it. It is to accept that we can only live under the sovereign rule of God, when we see all things as coming from Him and belonging to Him. The redemption of the world is only possible when we accept who the true owner is, for whom it is to be redeemed.

Whether rich or poor in material things we shall not inherit the kingdom if we are not poor in spirit. The rich man who is not detached becomes self-sufficient, insensitive to the needs of others and may be unjust. The poor man becomes covetous, bitter and envious. To be detached is to affirm the essential goodness of creation; it is to proclaim that in Christ it can be redeemed and come to its full potential to the glory of God.

CHAPTER XXVI

'BLESSED are those who mourn, for they shall be comforted.' To mourn is to weep, and the Lord, as the Gospels tell us, wept on two occasions. As He drew near and saw the city of Jerusalem, He wept over it, saying 'Would that even to-day you knew the things that make for peace! But now are they hid from your eyes.' Jesus wept before the tomb of Lazarus. On the first occasion He mourns because they have rejected the Author of life. He mourns not for Himself. 'Weep not for me but for yourselves and for your children.' He mourns because He knows that man created in the image of God is created for eternal fellowship with God. He mourns because man prefers to live alone with himself. At the tomb of Lazarus He mourns in compassion with those who have lost their brother. He also mourns because the death of Lazarus is the manifestation of the death which comes to everyman, and which apart from God is a death with no resurrection. 'The wages of sin is death.' The inevitable result of our refusal to accept our dependence upon God is the ultimate isolation of ourselves which is hell. 'But the gift of God is eternal life.'

Our Lord is not content merely to mourn. He who came to bring eternal life goes to endure the wages of sin, to suffer the desolation in death of man apart from God. He mourns in compassion, a true compassion which suffers to overcome. So He can say 'Be of good cheer, for I have overcome the world'. He who mourned for all mankind is comforted, for He is raised from the dead victorious to bring to men eternal life.

So the Christian mourns for the world. In Christ, he will mourn with love and in hope. He must not mourn in the way of the world with the grief of despair. Perhaps the greatest danger to-day is that he will mourn with the spirit of bitterness and look for consolation in a way which evades the cross. Instead of mourning in Christian hope there is the mourning of discontent. Those who mourn in that way will not be comforted, and for two reasons. First because it is a mourning which does not spring from love and from a desire that men may be reconciled and healed. It is possible to mourn because our ease and complacency are affronted. Secondly because such mourning does not recognise the true cause of the grief. Instead of facing the need to die to live, we clutch at ways which offer a cheap remedy. 'If only'—when we use these words, we are on the path which leads to spiritual death. We are not called to live and serve God in a situation which does not exist, and which, if it were to come, would enable us to live and serve Him while continuing in our self-centredness. When we live as if this were the case, we become bitter and blame others for their share in creating the conditions, which, so we believe, makes it so difficult for us to love God.

To mourn for the world without bitterness is a mark of the Christian. He is comforted in his mourning by the victory of Christ in which he is called to share and which he is to proclaim with loving sensitivity. In Christ he is to give unto them beauty for ashes, the oil of joy for mourning, the garment of praise for the spirit of heaviness.

CHAPTER XXVII

'BLESSED are the meek for they shall inherit the earth.' The quality of meekness is perhaps, of all the Christian qualities, that which is most unintelligible to the world. True, it is often confused with weakness and is, therefore, regarded as a quality to be despised. But even when meekness is seen in its strength, it is still unpopular. It is, therefore, at first sight, strange that of all the Beatitudes, it is that which speaks of meekness which also refers to 'inheriting the earth'. The reason, however, is not far to seek. Meekness embodies the willingness not to try and justify oneself. Trying to justify oneself is, as we have seen, essentially the way of the world.

The meek man has new characteristics. First, he is prepared to leave the justification of himself in God's hands. He is willing to lay his cause into the hands of 'him who judgeth righteously'. He accepts his dependence upon God and, responding in trust to the love of God, does what he believes to be required of him and leaves the issue with God. The temptations which our Lord endured in the wilderness were, in some sense, temptations not to be meek and to justify Himself. To have turned the stones into bread; to cast Himself from the temple and be saved dramatically; to be the declared earthly ruler of the nations; these are all temptations to do something which would have clearly established Him as justified in the world's eyes. Our Lord rejects them for it is not the way of God to force men to believe. His way is to win the allegiance of free men by suffering in love. Much of the weakness of the Church to-day springs from a desire to justify itself to the world on the world's terms. Show yourself concerned in social welfare; fight for racial justice; make the Church an efficient organisation by modern standards; when these concerns spring from our belief in the value of human life and the purpose of God for man, from our real compassion and understanding, all is well. Too often they spring to-day from impatience with the way of the Gospel and a desire to be accepted by the world as doing something which the world regards as worthwhile.

The second characteristic of the meek man is that he knows he cannot possess anything except by detachment and love. If he seeks to grasp his ability, his talents, his possessions for himself that he may be established, he is left unsatisfied. If he accepts them as in the ownership of God who has given them to him to be used in trust, he finds he truly possesses them, for he is enabled to fulfil himself. The meek man knows that he cannot gain the affection or allegiance of others except by love which abides for ever. Those who have seized others by violence or injustice or bought them with money will lose them. It is when we seek first the Kingdom of God and His righteousness, that all these things will be ours as well.

CHAPTER XXVIII

'BLESSED are those who hunger and thirst after righteousness, for they shall be satisfied.' Elsewhere our Lord tells us that unless our righteousness exceeds that of the Scribes and Pharisees, we will never enter the kingdom of heaven. The difference, however, is one of quality not quantity.

To live righteously is to live in loving and generous obedience to the sovereign rule of God, the Creator of the Universe. Both through our experience as human beings and through the moral demands revealed in the Old Testament, we are given knowledge of what scripture calls the Law—the will of God for His creation. Through our knowledge of the Law we are to be brought to dependence upon our Lord that we may be enabled to obey it. But in the hands of fallen men the Law became an instrument of man's self-sufficiency. Not that the Law was bad. Our Lord came not to destroy the Law but to fulfil it. The Law became an instrument of sin when men imagined that by scrupulous obedience to the Law, they could justify themselves in the sight of God. But not only must our attitude to God be one of surrender in love; if we seek to obey the Law as a means of self-personification we shall fail even to obey it in the spirit. The Law, which should bring us to repentance, is to be obeyed by fulfilment in love. There is, as it were, no resting-place of mere obedience. We can only obey the law by transcending obedience in love—and if our love is true love, it will embody and transcend obedience.

Our Lord alone has obeyed the Law by transcending it in love. His righteousness is the only true righteousness, for He died victorious over the temptations to justify Himself. His obedience to the Law and His fulfilment of it are consummated by His committal of Himself wholly into the Father's hands.

The Christian, living in Christ, hungers and thirsts after the righteousness of Christ. He does not seek a righteousness of his own apart from Christ. He can only receive the righteousness of Christ if he dies to the desire to seek one of his own. The desire for our own righteousness can take many forms. There was a time when it took the form of obedience to the moral law. 'Why should this happen to me? I've always lived a respectable life. Surely I deserve better than this?' Other kinds of expression are found to-day.

Involvement in social action or in the domestic affairs of the Church can come under the condemnation of righteousness by the Law if it is undertaken in the spirit of 'This makes me all right as a Christian'. That this is sometimes the case is seen by the exclusive spirit which is made evident. When we seek a righteousness of our own, we become censorious and sometimes bitter towards those who do not accept our criterion of righteousness. Further, we undermine the Gospel for we restrict righteousness to those who have the temperament or ability to fulfil our criterion or who live in circumstances which make it possible of fulfilment.

As we hunger and thirst for the righteousness of Christ we are satisfied in the measure which enables us to love and serve God as truly ourselves. 'There are varieties of gifts . . . all these are inspired by one and the same spirit who apportions to each one individually as he wills' (1 Cor. 12 : 7 and 11).

'Having gifts that differ according to the grace given to us, let us use them' (Rom. 12 : 6). The righteousness of Christ is given to us that we may be the salt of the earth and the light of the world. It is not given to us to hoard—to be buried in the earth.

CHAPTER XXIX

'BLESSED are the merciful for they shall obtain mercy.' At first sight some of the Beatitudes appear to have an air of spiritual bargaining. We must be merciful, the Lord seems to tell us, because otherwise we shall not receive mercy ourselves. That we should be tempted so to interpret them is a measure of our need to be converted. To try to be merciful or pure in heart or pure in spirit for what we may expect to get out of it is to be guilty of the sin of trying to use God for our own ends. We must recognise the Beatitudes for what they are. They are, as has been said, statements about the qualities which a Christian man should exhibit in his life. But they are more; they are the statements of the basic laws of spiritual life and growth. We are to be merciful because we are to be the kind of people who reflect the qualities which came from God, of which mercy is one. Being merciful, we shall be blessed, because to be merciful means that we shall obtain mercy.

To live as a Christian is to live perpetually under the mercy. We are what we are because we have accepted the mercy of God towards us. Our adoption as the sons of God 'accepted in the Beloved' is the work of the Father of mercies. Work is the right word for Scripture makes it plain that to show mercy is to act creatively for the restoration of the unhappy and sinful. To show mercy is not simply to overlook an injury or to wipe the slate clean.

When Saint Paul appeals to Christians 'through the mercies of God' to offer their bodies, their very selves to God as an act of intelligent worship, he is referring to all that God has done in the Life, Passion, Death and Resurrection of Christ. He is also referring to the all-embracing and merciful relationship into which we have been brought through the work of Christ and within which we are enabled, by the continuing mercy of God, to grow into all that God wants us to be.

As we live under the mercy, so we must show mercy.

Indeed, if we are truly living under the mercy, we shall show mercy and whether we do so or not is a test of whether we are living in that spirit or not. It is not simply a matter of duty, though duty must carry us along when our disposition to be merciful fails us. Nor is it just a question of performing 'works of mercy' though our mercy must find its expression in concrete acts.

To be merciful towards others demands a willingness to forgive and to bear the cost of forgiveness. It also demands that we seek to stretch out to others in a continuing spirit of healing and reconciliation. To be merciful is at one and the same time to be both realistic and optimistic; realistic, because we recognise the need of the person to whom we are to be merciful and optimistic, because the purpose of mercy is to enable the other person to be healed and truly to be himself.

One point needs to be stressed at the present time. Christians must begin by showing mercy to each other. Some Christians seem to find it easier to forgive the world than their fellow-Christians. But as judgment must begin in the household of God, so must forgiveness. I am thinking of this in two respects. First in terms of the life of the local worshipping community which should, by the exercise of mutual forgiveness, enable its members to grow in holiness. Secondly, in terms of the reform of the Church. When reform is in the air, as it is to-day, Christians will differ in their ideas of where it is needed and what form it should take. Such differences must be faced honestly and frankly, but they must be dealt with in a spirit of mutual forebearance and understanding and without personal rancour. Christians should be able to argue passionately in a desire to be obedient to God's truth without making issues a matter of their own personal vindication.

CHAPTER XXX

'BLESSED are the pure in heart for they shall see God.' To be pure in heart is to be single-minded. It is to have a vision which we pursue with the whole of our being. To speak of pursuing a vision does not contradict what has been said earlier about our dependence upon God and the fact that living as a Christian is always a response to what God has done for us. When we have accepted our dependence upon Him, we then have to bring every part of our being under His sovereign rule. Our minds have to be exercised to the fullest extent of their ability to understanding the inspiration of what God has done for us. Our bodies have to be brought under discipline so that we are not at the mercy of every instinct or passion and can use them in obedience to God. Our emotions have to be controlled so that they inspire our love of God and not our self-centredness.

Our difficulty is that we do not really believe that what God wants is infinitely the best thing for us. The reason is partly because we have a dim and limited vision of what He wants us to be. Man is made in the image of God. Our Lord lived, died and rose again so that men might be enabled to live as those who reflect God's image and do so not just out of duty as His servants but lovingly and generously as His sons. Holy Scripture speaks to us of God who creates with prodigious generosity. It spcaks of God of infinite splendour and glory. It speaks of God who is the source of all goodness and integrity. It speaks of God who is utterly consistent and to be trusted. It speaks of God who wants us to love Him freely and joyfully. It speaks of God who when we abuse the freedom He gives, acts with inexhaustible love and mercy. The picture given to us in the book of Revelation is one of the joyful, almost abandoned, adoration of God by the whole of Creation truly being itself.

What a contrast this is with our narrow, inhibited idea of holiness. For many people the Christian life implies restriction, suppressions and denial of what is human. The trouble is that we do not like hard work as far as the spiritual life is concerned. We sometimes try and conceal this implacable truth by talking of sincerity and not being true to ourselves. The plain fact is that any really worth while act is achieved through single-mindedness and hard work, whether it be in the realm of craftsmanship, service, music, the pictorial arts or any significant human activity. I may amuse myself at odd moments by dabbling at the piano, but I cannot acquire the satisfaction of being able to play the works of the great composers spontaneously and with understanding unless I accept the discipline of the art and apply myself to it.

'For now we see in a mirror dimly but, then, face to face.' To see God and to enjoy His presence in eternity demands here and now the steady single-minded application of ourselves in His service. The vision which inspires us to such application is given in Christ who is ever set before us in the Word of Scripture and the Sacrament of the Eucharist. By faithfulness in our use of these immediate signs of the Presence of our Lord, our vision is strengthened and renewed and our will to persevere fortified.

CHAPTER XXXI

'BLESSED are the peacemakers for they shall be called the sons of God.' For most people to-day, peace simply means the absence of war and strife. In the Old Testament it has a much more positive and deeper meaning. If we are to use one word to try and convey this meaning, harmony is probably the best we can use. Peace is the state of harmony which results when creation is established in a right relationship to God. It was for this reason that the prophets in the Old Testament have to distinguish between true peace which springs from the reconciliation of man and thereby of creation to God and false peace which is sought apart from God. So Jeremiah says 'For from the least to the greatest of them, every one is greedy for unjust gain; and from prophet to priest, everyone deals falsely. They have healed the wound of my people lightly, saying, "Peace, peace", when there is no peace' (Jeremiah 6 : 13, 14).

It was for this reason also that our Lord spoke of the peace which He came to bring and which He gives to His disciples and at the same time said that He did not come to bring peace but a sword. True peace and harmony come when a man accepts his dependence upon God and his need for reconciliation. Our Lord in His own Person, presented and still presents this truth in its uncompromising starkness, and so men rejected and continue to reject Him.

Through Christ, 'who is our peace', we are brought into a state of peace with God. It is peace which is to be shared in the common life of the Church. So Saint Paul, having spoken of the peace which our Lord has made possible through the Cross, speaks of us as fellow citizens with the saints and members of the household of God. He begs us (Eph. 4 : 1–3) to lead a life worthy of the calling to which we have been called, with patience, forbearing one another in love, eager to maintain the unity of the Spirit in the bond of peace. It is as we learn to live in the community of peace that we are enabled to bring every aspect of our nature, our skills and possessions under the sovereign rule of God. When the various aspects of our nature are not so directed, they tend to spring apart and become ends in themselves. So love becomes lust. The proper instinct to rest becomes sloth. A concern for truth becomes harsh dogmatism. But as God rules us, so there is harmony with each aspect of our life contributing its own part to the whole.

Christians are not merely to be men of peace. We are to be peacemakers. We are, as Saint Peter says, to seek peace and pursue it. In so doing, we live worthily of this vocation as sons of God. In Christ, the True Son, we are enabled to make the true response to the Father, living in generous loving obedience and bringing harmony where there is strife and disintegration.

We must begin in our family of the Church. We must learn to speak the truth in love, so that by a deepening obedience to the truth of God, we grow in harmony. Accepting Christ as the true and only source of peace and growing together with Him who is the Head, we are enabled to make peace in the world. Our love for our neighbour in the pew and our desire to live in peace with him is a test of our love for our neighbour in the world. If we profess to love our neighbour in the world, be he hungry, homeless, or racially oppressed, and hate our neighbour in the pew, we must ask ourselves if the peace we are seeking to make in the world is the true peace rooted in the love of God.

CHAPTER XXXII

'BLESSED are those who are persecuted for righteousness' sake for theirs is the kingdom of heaven.' At first sight, our Lord appears to be speaking of those who are subjected to action at the hands of others and not of those who show a quality of life. But He does not say that all who are persecuted are blessed. It is those who are persecuted for righteousness' sake to whom He refers and they must have the quality of being prepared to put the claims of God, of trust and conscience before their own case.

Our Lord then immediately applies this Beatitude to the disciples personally: 'Blessed are you when men revile you and persecute you'. The world will no more welcome those who show the qualities of the Christian any more than it welcomes Christ. When these qualities were perfectly embodied in the person of our Lord, men set upon Him and killed Him. He presented the ultimate challenge—dependence upon God or self-sufficiency and the powers of evil did their utmost to overcome Him.

If we are to be faithful to our Christian discipleship we must take the measure of the forces against us. The problems of the world are not, in the last resort, simply caused by ignorance or bad administration. We face problems of violence, poverty, bad housing and war because men are violent, grasping, unjust, greedy and bitter. While, as Christians, we must do all that we can to take our part in remedying the situations which arise because of what is in man, we must also proclaim boldly and without fear that the real solution lies in the re-creation of men and women in Christ. It is when we do this that we become conscious of the truth of Saint Paul's words: 'We wrestle not against flesh and blood but against the principalities, against the forces, against the rulers of this present darkness, against the spiritual hosts of wickedness in the heavenly places'.

This is not the place to discuss the philosophical problem

of evil. What we must do is to follow the example of our Lord who makes it clear that we shall never take the measure of evil if we do not think in terms of conscious powers of evil who seek to force the issue at every turn, tempting us away from dependence upon God.

The Lord has won the victory upon the Cross by accepting all that the powers of evil could bring to bear upon Him, yet remaining unbroken in His allegiance to the Father. But we have to reap the fruits of His victory by our conscious free allegiance to Christ, and by appealing to our free will the forces of evil can force a conflict.

The ways of the devil are very subtle. While he can tempt us to an obvious and major downfall, he seems much more disposed to deal in another way with those who are seeking to respond to the love of God. He seeks to spoil and corrupt the good we seek rather than take evil and intensify it. So, if we are not careful, we find our compassion slipping into condonation and our concern for the world becoming acceptance of its way. Our proper desire to be sincere is corrupted into a soft sentimentality or a state in which our feelings become paramount. We arrive at that state of mind in which to engage in dialogue is regarded as much more Christian than being persecuted for righteousness' sake.

CHAPTER XXXIII

THAT the Christian life involves a warfare with evil is made clear by the life of our Lord. From the moment of His Baptism when He was anointed with the Holy Spirit for His Mission, until the event of His Resurrection, His life falls into two parts. First there is what we call the Public Ministry, when He went about teaching, healing, and doing all manner of good among the people. During this time He was also concerned to train the disciples for the mission which they would have to execute in His name. His work at this stage was limited, humanly speaking, to those with whom He came into contact as He walked through the villages and fields of Palestine.

His mission was not, however, to be limited to the few. He did not come simply to be an example. He came to redeem the whole of mankind and in His person to re-create human nature. This He was to achieve through His Passion, Death and Resurrection. So there came the moment when He said 'Behold, we go up to Jerusalem'. It was the moment from which He went forward to defeat the powers of evil. He described the moment as 'this hour' but also as 'his hour'. It was their hour for they were to do with Him as they willed. He was to accept the worst they could bring upon Him. It was also to be His hour for it was to culminate in the moment of His victory, when, the powers of evil having done their worst, they could not break His loving obedience to the Father.

Our Lord went forward to accept misunderstanding, ridicule, betrayal, false accusations, being forsaken by His followers, scourging and finally the last weapon of evil—death. Our Lord died as we shall die, taking the last step alone. But He died 'trusting to him who judges justly'. He lays His life, His whole cause, into the Father's hands; confident that He will not, as the Psalmist says, 'leave his soul in Hades nor suffer his holy one to see corruption'.

When Saint Peter speaks of our Lord's work in these terms

he begins by telling us that He suffered for us, leaving us an example that we should follow in His steps. 'He committed no sin—no guile was found on his lips. When he was reviled he did not revile in return; when he suffered he did not threaten: but he trusted in him who judges justly. He himself bore our sins in his body on the tree that we might die to sin and live to righteousness' (1 Peter 2 : 22–24).

As Christians we are called to reap the fruit of Christ's work of redemption and re-creation. But all healing and reconciling work done in His name must be based upon the mastery of evil. The Public Ministry of our Lord must be seen in the light of His Passion, Death and Resurrection. He, Himself, shows how the teaching about social relationships, about marriage, about justice in our dealings with one another, about our use of the earth's resources, can only be put into effect if we are prepared to die to sin—to our self-centredness—and live as those who share His risen life.

As Christians we are all called to practise the way of exchange. We have to allow the evil which comes to us, whether through our own folly or that of others, to spend itself within us. When evil comes to us, it can either find some response such as bitterness, resentment, unholy indignation springing from self-righteousness or lack of charity, or it can spend itself within us, there to be exchanged for trust in God, compassion and love. In the former case, we have added to the evil in the world; we have helped to disseminate its corrupting influence. In the latter case, we have by the grace of God, helped to redeem it.

CHAPTER XXXIV

IT is when our life as Christians is based upon the way of exchange that our activities of healing, reconciling, teaching or bringing relief, can be delivered from both the spirit of patronising and harsh condemnation and from the false and unkind condonation of sin. We fail in our vocation if, while feeding the hungry or housing the homeless, we pour out bitterness and resentment against those who produce the hunger or the overcrowding.

If we are to live the way of exchange one thing is essential. We must ourselves be learning to live as those who are perpetually under the mercy. We must know ourselves to be those who have been accepted by God as we are and are forgiven.

We must also remember that evil is at root to be dealt with by spiritual weapons. We may deal with its symptoms in physical ways, but dealing with the symptoms must not become a substitute for the conquest of evil itself. Neither must we imagine that in the domestic life of the Church reforms of structures or administration will, by themselves, produce holiness and equip the Church for mission. The introduction of synodical government, for example, may be absolutely right and give us the framework in which the Church together can learn the mind of Christ. But its effectiveness will depend upon whether we use the opportunities it gives to learn to conquer temptations, to suspicion and bitterness, and to grow in love and humility.

What are the spiritual weapons? Prayer, and learning to bring the body under control of the Holy Spirit are two essential ones. In prayer we draw upon the power of the risen, victorious Christ. In learning to control our bodies we are delivered from being at the beck and call of our instincts and passions. We do well to remember some words of Canon Roger Lloyd who wrote 'The rewards of an evil act are paid at once and on the spot, whereas the transactions of good are generally on a long-credit basis. It is the difference between lust and love. Anyone can lust; it is the easiest thing in the world and its rewards are both pleasurable and immediate. Love, too, presents a haunting image to the imagination; but love, being a settled disposition of the mind, can give its rewards only to a mind steadily disciplined and purged.'[1] It must also be remembered that to give in to lust makes us weaker for the next temptation, whereas to resist means that we shall be just that bit more chaste to face it.

'A mind steadily disciplined and purged.' The strength of our will depends to a large extent on the vision of the objective which we have. We need continually to be nourished by a deeper understanding of God's purpose for us and of the splendour and glory of the holiness to which we are called. For this reason, regular reading of Scripture is an essential spiritual weapon. Having Scripture at our finger-tips, as it were, enables us in moments of temptation to recall the nature and demands of the Christian life and fortifies us to resist.

[1] R. Lloyd, *The Mastery of Evil,* Centenary Press, revised edition, 1944, p. 29.

CHAPTER XXXV

THE Prologue in the Bible gives us the setting in which we are to understand the Biblical history of our redemption. The Epilogue, which is the Book of Revelation, gives us the end-point. Here, in the most dramatic and, at times, mysterious language, we are given a vision of the ultimate purpose for which creation exists. It is the gathering together of all things in one even in Christ of which Saint Paul speaks in his letter to the Church at Ephesus. We see the whole of creation set in a new relationship to God. Every part, freed from the bondage of corruption, perfectly fulfils itself and does so to the glory of God. Man, as the vice-gerent of creation, takes his place in expressing the praises of creation as it reflects back to God His Holiness. In the Prologue is the story of the Tower of Babel where man is pictured as trying to build for himself a civilisation which would justify itself apart from God and the result is chaos and confusion. In the Epilogue the holy city comes down from heaven. It is the result of the divine activity of love, so that man may live with God in creation perfectly redeemed and fulfilled.

It has often been pointed out that the Bible begins with a garden and ends with a city. That is true but it is a garden city in which the tree of life occupies a central place, in which nature and man's use of nature are redeemed and united in the sphere of man's eternal communion with God.

Now creation is opaque. There are dark places and the glory of God is obscured by the self-centredness of man and his misuse of creation. Creation does not reflect back to God His Beauty, Order, Majesty and Love. But in Christ man can be redeemed and can then learn to take his part in making creation the sphere of communion with God. In one sense, it is as if we are occupied in the cleaning of an old master, removing the grime so that the beauty of the painting may shine through, which will speak to us of the painter himself. But the illustration is very inadequate for the painter does not keep us to clean the painting. Nor is the purpose of the operation that in and through the painting we may live in a personal relationship with the painter. God enables us to purify and redeem His creation so that in and through it, we may live in communion with Him.

The fellowship which we are given with God in Christ here and now to be lived out in obedience and suffering is not to be limited to this world. It is to be fulfilled in the world to come at the 'end of the age'. Time will be no more for we shall be caught up into the ceaseless and eternal life of God which is both perfect activity and perfect rest.

Of this we can only speak while stammering for words. Yet we are given glimpses of what shall be. Here and now there are moments when time stands still. The craftsman working with his hands; the lover with his beloved; the ordinary man called to perform an act of heroic compassion; such know what it is to forget the time and to forget themselves being wholly absorbed in their actions. Yet afterwards they will say, 'This was a moment when I was being myself'.

In Christ we are to be occupied in the perfect exercise of the whole of our being to the glory of God. We shall forget ourselves in Him yet we shall be truly ourselves, expressing with all the saints what is the breadth and length and height and depth of the love of Christ which surpasses knowledge that we may be filled with all the fulness of God.